Contents

Introduction

In this book I have combined two things that have played a large part in my life – sugarcraft and cats. I have kept the modelling as easy as possible, using just a few items of equipment, while still trying to give each model a different character. Although I have used modelling paste, these cats could also be made using

Twenty to Make
Sugar Cats

Frances McNaughton

Search Press

First published 2016

Search Press Limited
Wellwood, North Farm Road,
Tunbridge Wells, Kent TN2 3DR

Text copyright © Frances McNaughton 2016

Photographs by Paul Bricknell at
Search Press Studios

Photographs and design copyright
© Search Press Ltd 2016

Print ISBN: 978-1-78221-287-4
eBook ISBN: 978-1-78126-314-3

Suppliers
If you have difficulty in obtaining any of the
materials and equipment mentioned in this book,
then please visit the Search Press website for
details of suppliers: www.searchpress.com

Printed in China

Dedication
To my family and friends who have all supported me
while writing my books over the last few years.

marzipan, modelling chocolate or non-edible modelling pastes. The sizes of the models can be changed easily; the weights given are for guidance only, and with a little experience and experimentation you will soon be able to make all sorts of different feline characters in many colours and poses.

When I had a larger garden, I used to help my local cat rescue charity by fostering cats and kittens waiting for new homes. Some of the names I have chosen for the cats in this book relate to children, people and, of course, some of the cats I have known.

I am also a proud guardian of three cats who still often behave like kittens, even though they are not. Watching them has helped me choose the variety of poses shown in the sugar cats here.

I hope you have as much fun as I did making the cats for this book.

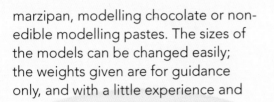

Materials and tools

Materials

Modelling paste is used for the main parts of the cats. It can be made by kneading 5ml (one teaspoon) of CMC/Tylose into 500g (1lb) of commercial fondant (sugarpaste). It is also available ready-made.

Fondant (sugarpaste) works well for making long fur and fluff. It can be blended and textured, as it stays soft for longer than modelling paste.

Edible ink felt-tip pen This is used for drawing paw pads onto the feet.

Paint palette This is used for mixing colours.

Edible food colour powders can be brushed on dry or mixed with vodka or water for painting on detail.

Tiny, white, edible sugar pearls make very good tiny teeth.

Small, black, edible sugar pearls are perfect for cats' eyes. Buy them, or make a few in advance using black modelling paste and allow to dry. Glaze them using confectioner's varnish.

Other items not shown:

Food grade alcohol/vodka This is mixed with edible food colour powders for painting markings on the cats.

Vegetable cooking oil Use this sparingly on your workboard, tools and hands to stop the paste sticking.

Icing sugar Use only if necessary (it can cause cracking if too much is used) when working to stop the paste sticking.

> **Tip:** When sticking any parts together, brush water on sparingly with a small paintbrush to make the surface tacky, but not wet. The sugar should then be sticky enough to attach. If water does not stick the pieces together, or if you have breakages, use a small amount of whichever paste you are trying to stick, mix it with a small amount of water using a palette knife until it is stringy, and use it as a gluey filler between the pieces. This is also known as 'gunge'.

Tools

Non-stick workboard

A pair of **small, sharp, pointed scissors** is used for cutting paste and snipping details.

Push paste through a **tea strainer or small sieve** to make fur and fluff.

A **water brush (or paintbrush)** will be needed to dampen modelling paste ready for sticking.

A **small paintbrush** is used for painting on edible food colour powder for markings.

A **dogbone tool or small ball tool** is used for modelling the paste.

Use a **Dresden tool** to make indents for eyes and noses and for creating texture.

Release your models from the work surface with a **small, fine palette knife** and also use it to create texture or marks.

Use a **ruler** to measure pieces of paste.

A **small, non-stick rolling pin** is used to roll out modelling paste.

Small foam pieces are good for supporting pieces of modelling paste while they are drying.

Store pieces of paste in **plastic sandwich bags** to keep them soft.

Weigh the modelling paste with some **cheap jewellery scales** for accuracy.

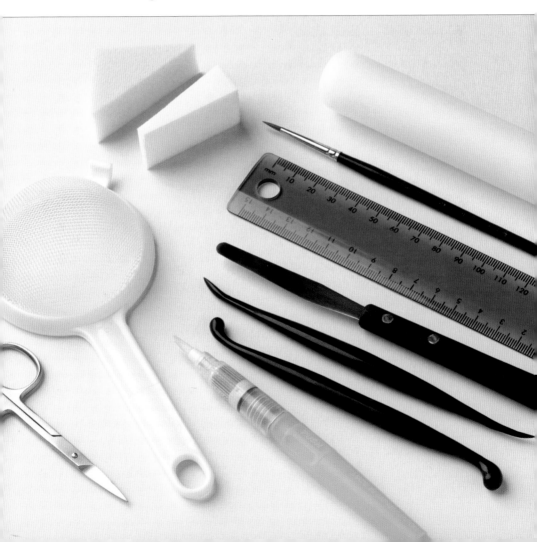

Kiki

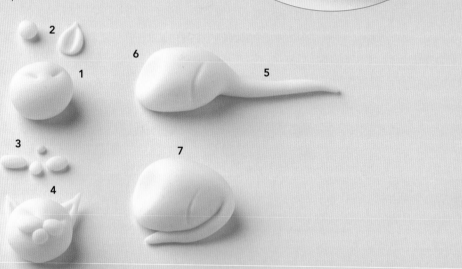

Materials:

15g (½oz) white or cream modelling paste

Tiny piece of pink fondant (sugarpaste)

Orange food colour powder

Vodka for painting

Tools:

Dresden tool

Small paintbrush

Instructions:

1 Shape 5g ($^1/_6$oz) of modelling paste into a ball and mark two lines for the eyes using the Dresden tool.

2 Make two ears by shaping very small balls into pointed cone shapes and press the wide end of the Dresden tool in to make a dip in the middle. Dampen and attach to the back of the head.

3 Make two very small ovals of paste for the cheeks, one small ball for the chin and shape a tiny piece of pink fondant (sugarpaste) for the nose.

4 Attach all four pieces to the face.

5 Shape the rest of the paste (about 10g/$^1/_3$oz) into a ball to make the body, and then roll one end firmly to form the tail. The overall length will be about 7cm (2¾in).

6 Press your finger in at the head end of the body to make a dip, and mark the back leg with the Dresden tool.

7 Curve the tail around the body.

8 Dampen the dip at the head end and attach the head to the body.

9 Use a dry paintbrush to brush orange food colour powder all over Kiki, except for her nose, cheeks and chin, which just need a very light dusting.

10 Mix a little of the food colour powder with a few drops of vodka, then paint on the stripes and the closed eyes, using the photographs above and opposite for guidance.

Kiki's comfy pillow can be made by shaping an oblong of fondant (sugarpaste) big enough for her to sleep on. Make a dip in the middle with your thumb, about the same shape and size as the cat. Roll out some fondant (sugarpaste) thinly and cut an oblong larger than the pillow, using it as a template. Lay the oblong over the pillow, pinch the corners and press into the middle again, forming creases if desired. Finally, dust with lavender pearl food colour powder.

Buffy

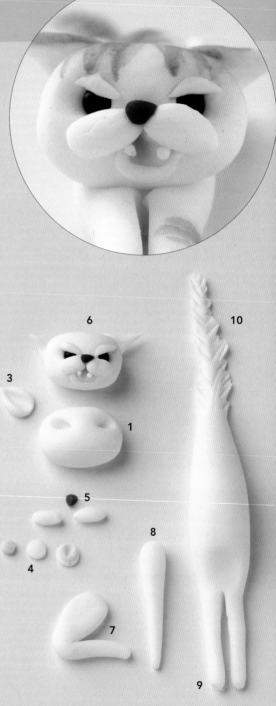

Materials:

20g (²/₃oz) white modelling paste

2 x black sugar pearls

2 x tiny white sugar pearls

Tiny piece of pink fondant (sugarpaste)

Tiny piece of brown fondant (sugarpaste)

Orange food colour powder

Vodka for painting

Tools:

Dresden tool

Small paintbrush

Small, fine palette knife

Instructions:

1 Shape 5g (¹/₆oz) of modelling paste into an oval for the head. Mark two holes for the eyes using the Dresden tool and insert the black sugar pearl eyes.

2 Make two tiny sausages for the eyebrows. Dampen the area above the eyes and attach them, angled downwards in the middle, to give Buffy an angry expression.

3 Make two ears as described on page 8. Dampen and attach the ears to the back of the head, so that they are pointing out to either side.

4 Make a small, pink ball of fondant (sugarpaste) for the tongue and a slightly larger white ball for the chin. Stick the pink ball on top of the chin, press it down with the Dresden tool and then attach it to the face.

5 Make two very small white ovals for the cheeks, and one small ball of brown fondant (sugarpaste) for the nose.

6 Attach the cheeks, followed by the tiny piece of brown paste for the nose. Dampen inside the mouth and attach the two white sugar pearls for the top teeth. Buffy's head is now complete.

7 Cut 3g (¹/₈oz) of paste in half and shape the back legs by making two 4cm (1½in) cones. Bend in the middle and flatten the wide end slightly. Mark three toes with the knife.

8 Shape the rest of the paste (about 12g/²/₅oz) into a ball, then roll one end firmly to form the tail and roll the other end for the front. Lengthen the body by rolling it in the palm of your hand. The overall length will be about 12cm (4¾in).

9 Cut 3cm (1¼in) into the front end of the body with the palette knife to make the front legs. Mark the toes as before. Make a dip for the head by pressing a finger in.

10 Make the tail look like long fur by marking it with the Dresden tool.

11 Dampen the dip and attach the head to the body.

12 Mix a little of the orange food colour powder with a few drops of vodka, then paint on Buffy's stripes.

Buffy is a feisty cat. Take care to angle his cheeks and eyebrows correctly to give him his characterful expression.

Carys

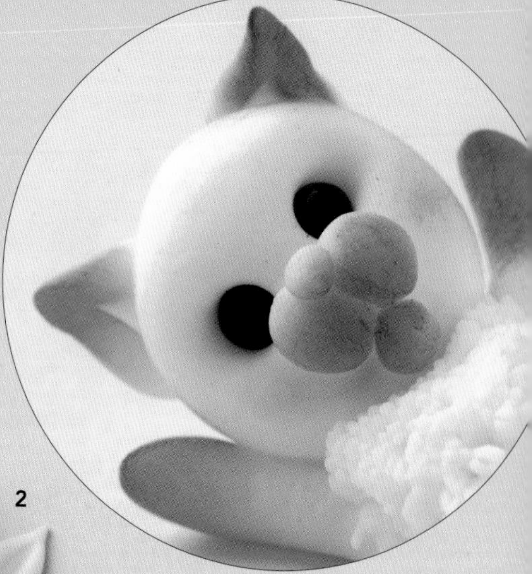

Materials:

15g (½oz) white modelling paste

Small amount of white fondant (sugarpaste)

Tiny piece of pink fondant (sugarpaste)

2 x black sugar pearls

Dark brown food colour powder

Tools:

Dresden tool

Small paintbrush

Small, fine palette knife

Tea strainer or small sieve

Instructions:

1 Shape 5g (⅙oz) of white modelling paste into a ball. Mark two holes for the eyes using the Dresden tool. Insert the black sugar pearl eyes.

2 Make two ears as described on page 8. Dampen and attach the ears to the back of the head.

3 Make three very small balls of fondant (sugarpaste) for the cheeks and chin, and a tiny ball of pink fondant (sugarpaste) for the nose.

4 Attach all four shapes to the cat's face.

5 Shape the rest of the paste (about 10g/⅓oz) into an oval, then pinch one end firmly to form a short tail.

6 Pinch and shape four small legs as shown. Twist the body to make it look like Carys is lying on her side with her front paws raised.

7 Press a finger in at the head end. Dampen the dip and attach the head.

8 Use a dry paintbrush to dust dark brown food colour powder over the paws, tip of the tail, ears, cheeks and chin.

9 Press a small amount of white fondant (sugarpaste) through the tea strainer or sieve to make fluff and cut it off with the knife. Dampen the chest and attach the fluff, pressing it gently into place with the pointed end of the Dresden tool to avoid flattening it.

Carys's playful pose makes her look very sweet. Make a couple of balls of coloured fondant (sugarpaste) for her to play with.

Katie

Materials:

20g (²/₃oz) white
modelling paste

Small amount of white
fondant (sugarpaste)

2 x black sugar pearls

Tiny piece of pink
fondant (sugarpaste)

Dark brown food
colour powder

Vodka for painting

Tools:

Dresden tool

Small paintbrush

Small, fine
palette knife

Tea strainer or sieve

Instructions:

1 To make the head, shape 5g (¹/₆oz) of modelling paste into an oval. Mark two holes for the eyes using the Dresden tool. Insert the black sugar pearl eyes.

2 Make two ears as described on page 8. 'Feather' down opposite edges by pressing with the Dresden tool. Dampen and attach to the back of the head, with the feathered edges outwards.

3 Make two small ovals of fluff for the cheeks by pressing a small amount of white fondant (sugarpaste) through the tea strainer or sieve. Cut the fluff off and attach to the face, as described on page 12. Shape one very small ball of white paste for the chin and attach in place. Make and attach a tiny pink nose.

4 Shape the rest of the modelling paste (about 10g/¹/₃oz) into a ball, roll one end firmly to form the tail and roll the other end for the front. Lengthen the body by rolling it in the palm of your hand. The overall length will be about 9cm (3½in).

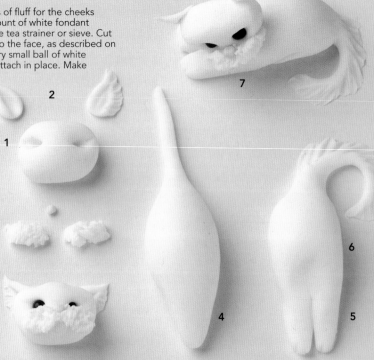

5 Cut 2cm (¾in) into the front end of the body with the palette knife for the front legs. Mark three toes on each foot with the knife. Mark the shape for the back leg using the Dresden tool.

6 Make a dip for the head by pressing a finger in. Make the tail look like long fur by marking it with the Dresden tool.

7 Dampen the dip and attach the head to the body.

8 Brush some dark brown food colour powder over Katie, avoiding her cheeks and nose, then mix a little of the powder with a few drops of vodka. Use this to paint on the stripes.

Katie's fluffy cheeks and tail make her very appealing. Give her an extra-wide expression by painting a sweeping line from the outside corners of her eyes, as shown below.

Rubydoo

Materials:

20g (²/₃oz) white
   modelling paste

2 x black sugar pearls

Tiny piece of pink
   fondant (sugarpaste)

Grey food colour powder

Pink edible ink
   felt-tip pen

Tools:

Dresden tool

Small paintbrush

Small, fine
   palette knife

Small foam pieces

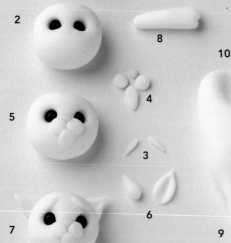

Instructions:

1 Shape 5g (¹/₆oz) of modelling paste into a ball. Mark two holes for the eyes using the Dresden tool.

2 Insert the black sugar pearl eyes into the holes.

3 Make two tiny sausages for the eyebrows from the modelling paste. Dampen the area above the eyes and attach them, angled upwards in the middle, to give Rubydoo a surprised expression.

4 Make two very small balls of paste for the cheeks, and one small cone for the chin. Then shape a tiny piece of pink fondant (sugarpaste) for the nose.

5 Attach all four shapes to the face.

6 Make two ears as described on page 8. Dampen and attach the ears to the back of the head.

7 Rubydoo's head is now complete.

8 Make the legs by cutting 3g (¹/₈oz) of modelling paste into four pieces. Shape them to form 2cm (¾in) cones. Press the knife in over the wide ends to mark three toes on each foot.

9 Shape the rest of the paste (about 10g/¹/₃oz) into a ball, then roll one end firmly to form the tail.

Lengthen the body by rolling it in the palm of your hand. The overall length will be about 6cm (2³/₈in).

10 Make a dip for the head by pressing a finger in.

11 Dampen the dip and attach the head to the body. Then attach the legs to the body. If necessary, prop up the legs and head until dry, using some foam pieces.

12 Brush some grey food colour powder over the kitten with a small paintbrush, leaving her paws, cheeks, chin and tummy white.

13 Draw Rubydoo's paw pads on using the pink felt-tip pen.

If you want to make a little blanket for Rubydoo to recline on, cut out a square of thinly rolled pink fondant (sugarpaste) and mark it with a stitching wheel and a zig-zag wheel. Then gently frill the edge with a cocktail stick or a frilling tool.

Colleen and Kittens

Materials:

30g (1oz) white
    modelling paste

5g (1/6oz) black
    modelling paste

2 x black sugar pearls

Tiny piece of pink
    fondant (sugarpaste)

Black and orange food
    colour powder

Vodka for painting

Tools:

Dresden tool

Small paintbrush

Small, fine
    palette knife

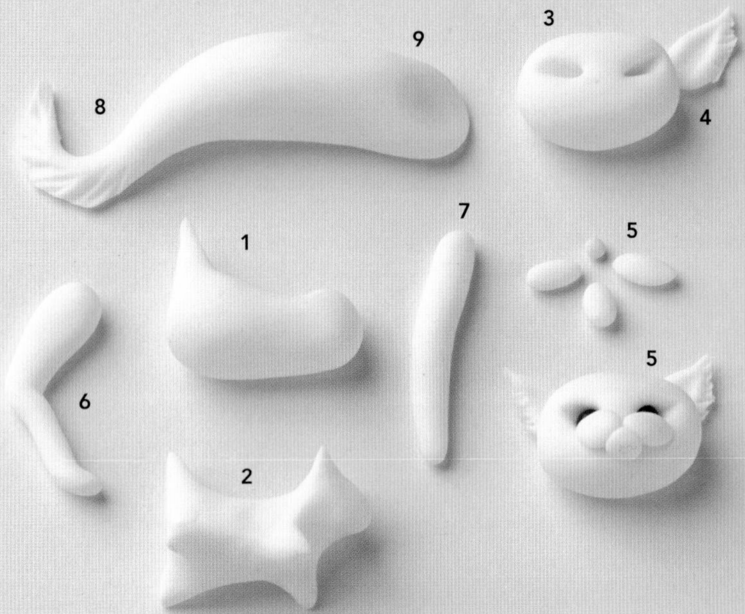

Instructions:

1 For each kitten, shape 5g (1/6oz) of modelling paste into an oval (two with white paste and one with black paste). Pinch a little pointed tail up at right angles.

2 Roll between your fingers to form a shape for the neck and head. Pinch up two pointed ears, then pinch and shape four short legs.

3 To make Colleen's head, shape 5g (1/6oz) of white modelling paste into an oval. Mark two holes for the eyes using the Dresden tool and insert the black sugar pearls for her eyes.

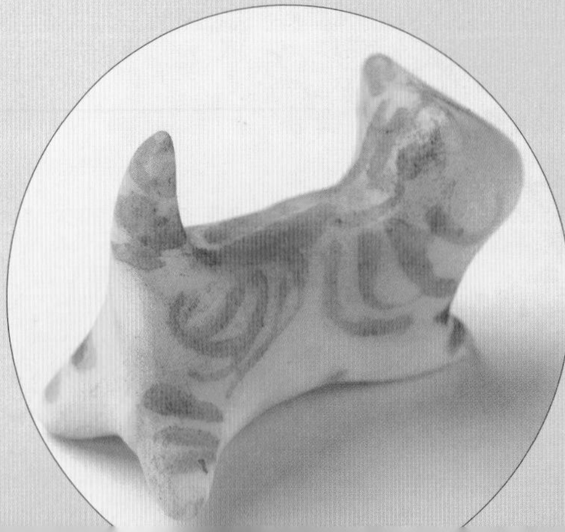

4 Make two ears as described on page 8. 'Feather' down the outside edges by pressing along them with the Dresden tool. Dampen and attach to the back of the head, with the feathered edges facing outwards.

5 Make three very small ovals of white paste for the cheeks and chin and attach to the face. Attach a tiny piece of pink fondant (sugarpaste) for the nose.

6 Cut a 5g (1/6oz) piece of white paste into four pieces, and shape the two back legs first by making two 4cm (1½in) cones. Bend them in the middle and flatten the wide end slightly.

7 Shape the front legs into 4cm (1½in) sausages. Mark three toes onto each foot with the knife.

8 Shape the rest of the paste (about 10g/1/3oz) into a ball, then roll one end firmly to form the tail. Lengthen the body by rolling it in the palm of your hand. The overall length will be about 10cm (4in).

9 Make a dip for the head by pressing a finger in. Make the tail look like long fur by marking it with the Dresden tool.

10 Dampen and attach one back leg and one front leg slightly under the body. Dampen the dip and attach the head to the body.

11 Mix a little of the powder colours with a few drops of vodka, then paint the markings on Colleen and the ginger kitten.

12 Position the kittens, sticking them into place if desired. Dampen and attach the two remaining legs to fit around the kittens.

Colleen is named after one of my own cats. Although she has never had kittens of her own, I like to think she would have had cute ones like these.

Harvey

Materials:

20g (²/₃oz) white modelling paste

Small amount of white fondant (sugarpaste)

2 x black sugar pearls

Tiny piece of black fondant (sugarpaste)

Grey food colour powder

Vodka for painting

Pink edible ink felt-tip pen

Tools:

Dresden tool

Small, fine palette knife

Small foam pieces

Small paintbrush

Tea strainer or small sieve

Instructions:

1 To make the head, shape 5g (¹/₆oz) of modelling paste into a ball. Mark two holes for the eyes with the Dresden tool and insert the black sugar pearl eyes.

2 Make two tiny sausages of paste for the eyebrows, dampen the area above the eyes and attach them, angled upwards in the middle, to give Harvey a surprised expression.

3 Make two ears as described on page 8. Dampen and attach the ears to the back of the head.

4 Make two very small ovals of paste for the cheeks, one small ball for the chin, and roll a tiny piece of black fondant (sugarpaste) for the nose.

5 Attach all four pieces to the face.

6 Cut a 5g (¹/₆oz) piece of paste into four pieces, and shape the two back legs by first making two 4cm (1½in) cones. Bend them in the middle and flatten the wide end slightly.

7 Shape the front legs into 3cm (1¼in) sausages. Mark three toes onto each foot with the knife.

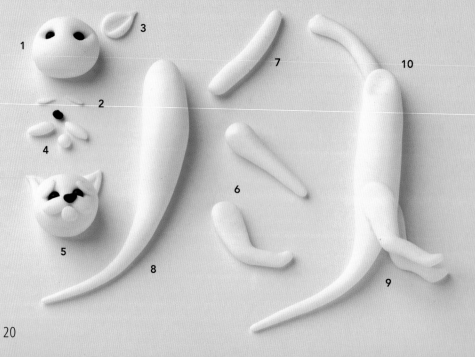

8 Shape the rest of the paste (about 10g/¹/₃oz) into a ball, then roll one end firmly to form the tail. Lengthen the body by rolling it in the palm of your hand. The overall length will be about 10cm (4in). Make a dip for the head by pressing a finger in.

9 Dampen and attach one back leg and one front leg slightly under the body. Position the tail and back in a straight line, with the body curving up at a right angle. Lay the cat across the corner of a square-edged board or piece of paper to make sure that the tail and back paws are in line and the body lines up against the other angle.

10 Dampen the dip at the front of the body and attach the head to the body.

11 Attach the other two legs, propping them apart with some small foam pieces. Leave to dry until hard. The two back legs and the tail will then form a steady 'tripod' to support the standing cat.

12 Brush some grey food colour powder over Harvey's back with a paintbrush. Mix a little of the powder with a few drops of vodka, then paint on the markings.

13 Press a small amount of white fondant (sugarpaste) through the tea strainer or small sieve. Cut the fluff off and attach it to Harvey's chest, as described on page 12.

14 Draw the pads on Harvey's forepaws using the pink felt-tip pen. Do not stand him up until he is completely dry.

Harvey is having a good stretch and probably sharpening his claws, too, as he stretches up this old tree trunk!

Eli

Materials:

20g (²/₃oz) white modelling paste

Small amount of white fondant (sugarpaste)

2 x black sugar pearls

Tiny piece of pink fondant (sugarpaste)

Tiny piece of brown fondant (sugarpaste)

Black food colour powder

Vodka for painting

Cocktail stick (optional)

Tools:

Dresden tool

Small paintbrush

Small, fine palette knife

Tea strainer or small sieve

Instructions:

1 Shape 5g (¹/₆oz) of white modelling paste into a ball. Mark two holes for the eyes using the Dresden tool and insert the black sugar pearl eyes.

2 Make two ears as described on page 8. Dampen and attach the ears to the back of the head.

3 Make two very small balls of paste for the cheeks, and one small oval of pink fondant (sugarpaste) for the tongue, marking a line down the centre. Then shape a tiny piece of brown fondant (sugarpaste) for the nose.

4 Attach the cheeks, tongue and nose to the face.

5 Cut a 5g (¹/₆oz) piece of paste into four pieces, and shape the two back legs first by making two 2cm (¾in) cones.

6 Shape the front legs into 4cm (1½in) sausages. Mark three toes onto all four feet with the knife.

7 Make a long, thin tail using a small piece of modelling paste.

8 Shape the rest of the paste (about 10g/¹/₃oz) to a cone about 3cm (1¼in) long. For extra support for the head, push a cocktail stick into the centre, but remember to warn people that there is a stick inside.

9 Attach the back legs and tail under the body.

10 Attach the head to the body, either by sticking or with the cocktail stick if used, tilting it to one side.

Stick the front legs on, with one paw raised over the lowest ear. Dampen to hold the paw in place.

11 Mix a little of the colour powder with a few drops of vodka, then paint on the black parts.

12 Press a small amount of white fondant (sugarpaste) through the tea strainer or small sieve. Cut the fluff off and attach it to Eli's chest, as described on page 12.

Eli is a cat full of charm and mischief, caught here having a wash.

Blanche

Materials:

20g (²/₃oz) white
modelling paste

10g (¹/₃oz) white fondant
(sugarpaste)

2 x black sugar pearls

Tiny piece of pink
fondant (sugarpaste)

Cocktail stick (optional)

Tools:

Dresden tool

Small paintbrush

Small, fine
palette knife

Tea strainer or
small sieve

Instructions:

1 Shape 5g (¹/₆oz) of modelling paste into a ball. Mark two holes widely apart for the eyes using the Dresden tool and insert the black sugar pearl eyes.

2 Make two ears as described on page 8. Dampen and attach to the back of the head.

3 Make two very small ovals of paste for the cheeks and one small ball for the chin. Dampen the face and attach with the cheeks tilting downwards. Make a tiny pink nose and stick it in place.

4 Blanche's head is now complete.

5 Make a long tail using a small piece of modelling paste.

6 Make the tail look like long fur by marking it with the Dresden tool.

7 Shape the rest of the paste (about 10g/¹/₃oz) into a cone about 3cm (1¼in) long for the body. For extra support for the head, push a cocktail stick into the centre, but remember to warn people that there is a stick inside.

8 Attach the tail under the body, then attach the head to the body

9 Press a small amount of white fondant (sugarpaste) through the tea strainer or small sieve, then cut the fluff off with the knife and put it into a small airtight container and repeat until you have enough to cover the whole cat. Begin attaching the fluff to Blanche's body, as described on page 12. Use the Dresden tool to press a space between the two front legs. Continue attaching fluff over the head until the whole cat is fluffy, leaving the cheeks and ears uncovered.

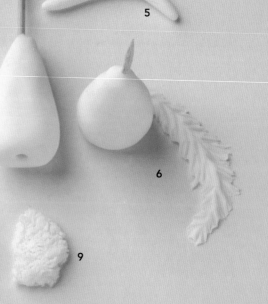

2

3

4

5

6

7

9

Blanche is the fluffiest of cats and, although her downward-sloping cheeks give her a rather grumpy expression, she has a very sweet nature!

Jack

Materials:

20g (²/₃oz) white modelling paste

Small amount of white fondant (sugarpaste)

2 x black sugar pearls

Tiny piece of black fondant (sugarpaste)

Pale brown food colour powder

Pink edible ink felt-tip pen

Cocktail stick (optional)

Tools:

Dresden tool

Paintbrush for dusting

Small, fine palette knife

Tea strainer or small sieve

Instructions:

1 Shape 5g (¹/₆oz) of modelling paste into a ball. Mark two holes for the eyes using the Dresden tool and insert the black sugar pearl eyes.

2 Make two ears as described on page 8. Dampen and attach the ears to the back of the head.

3 Make three very small pointed cone shapes of paste for the cheeks and chin, and a tiny black nose. Attach to the face.

4 Cut a 5g (¹/₆oz) piece of paste into four pieces, and shape the two back legs by making two 4cm (1½in) cones. Bend them in the middle and flatten the wide end slightly.

5 Shape the front legs into 3cm (1¼in) sausages. Mark three toes onto all four feet with the knife.

6 Shape the rest of the paste (about 10g/¹/₃oz) into a ball, then roll one end firmly to form the tail. Lengthen the body by rolling it in the palm of your hand. The overall length will be about 9cm (3½in). Bend it in the middle to form a right angle. To provide extra support for the head, push a cocktail stick through the main body, but remember to warn people that there is a stick inside. Support the body in an upright position while working on, and drying Jack.

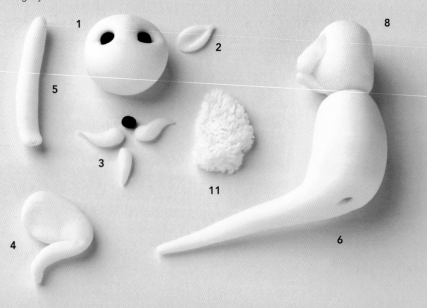

7 Dampen and attach the back legs so that Jack is sitting with his legs apart. Attach the front legs over his tummy.

8 Attach the head to the body.

9 Using the paintbrush, brush the food colour powder over the back, legs, head, ears, paws and tail.

10 Press a small amount of white fondant (sugarpaste) through the tea strainer or small sieve. Cut the fluff off and attach to the chest, as described on page 12.

11 Draw the pads on Jack's paws with the pink felt-tip pen.

Cats often sit like this when they are washing. Jack is a mischievous boy, but looks like butter wouldn't melt in his mouth.

Wannie

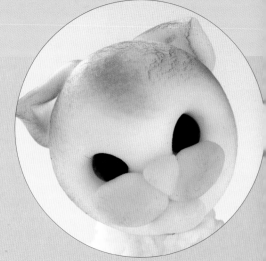

Materials:

20g (²/₃oz) white modelling paste

Small amount of white fondant (sugarpaste)

2 x black sugar pearls

Pale brown food colour powder

Pink edible ink felt-tip pen

Small sugar butterfly

Cocktail stick (optional)

Tools:

Dresden tool

Paintbrush for dusting

Small, fine palette knife

Tea strainer or small sieve

Small foam pieces

Instructions:

1 Shape 5g (¹/₆oz) of modelling paste into a ball. Mark two holes for the eyes using the Dresden tool and insert the black sugar pearl eyes.

2 Make two ears as described on page 8. Dampen and attach the ears to the back of the head.

3 Make three very small ovals of paste for the cheeks and chin, and a tiny piece of paste for the nose, then attach all four pieces to the face.

4 Wannie's head is now complete.

5 Cut a 5g (¹/₆oz) piece of paste into four pieces, and shape the two back legs first by making two 4cm (1½in) cones. Bend them in the middle.

6 Shape the front legs into 4cm (1½in) sausage shapes and bend one of them in the middle. Mark three toes onto all four feet with the knife.

7 Make a long, thin tail using a small piece of modelling paste.

8 Shape the rest of the paste (about 10g/¹/₃oz) into a cone about 4cm (1½in). If you want to provide extra support for the head, push a cocktail stick into the body, but remember to warn people that there is a stick inside.

9 Attach the back legs on either side of the body and the tail underneath.

10 Attach the head, tilting it to one side. Stick the front legs on, giving support to the bent, raised leg while it is drying.

11 Brush the pale brown food colour powder over Wannie's back, legs, head, ears, cheeks and tail.

12 Press a small amount of white fondant (sugarpaste) through the tea strainer or small sieve. Cut the fluff off and attach as described on page 12.

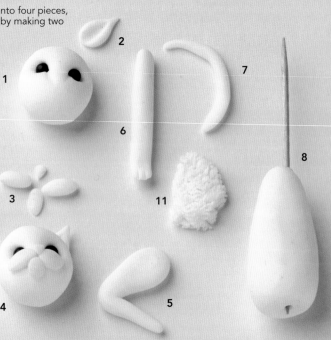

13 Draw the paw pads onto the raised front paw using the pink felt-tip pen. Attach the small sugar butterfly to Wannie's paw by mixing a tiny piece of 'gunge' (see page 6) and applying it to the underside of the butterfly.

Wannie is a whimsical cat who is fascinated by this butterfly and always loves to play.

Cattie

Materials:

20g (²/₃oz) white modelling paste

Small amount of white fondant (sugarpaste)

2 x black sugar pearls

Tiny piece of black fondant (sugarpaste)

Black and orange food colour powder

Vodka for painting

Tools:

Dresden tool

Small paintbrush

Small, fine palette knife

Small foam pieces

Instructions:

1 Shape 5g (¹/₆oz) of modelling paste into a ball. Mark two holes for the eyes using the Dresden tool and insert the black sugar pearl eyes.

2 Make two ears as described on page 8. Dampen and attach the ears to the back of the head.

3 Make three very small balls of modelling paste for the cheeks and chin, and shape a tiny piece of black fondant (sugarpaste) for the nose. Attach all four pieces to the face.

4 Cut a 5g (¹/₆oz) piece of modelling paste into four pieces, and shape the two back legs first by making two 4cm (1½in) cones. Bend them in the middle and flatten the wide end slightly.

5 Shape the front legs into 3cm (1¼in) sausages. Mark three toes onto each foot with the knife.

6 Shape the rest of the paste (about 10g/¹/₃oz) into a ball, then roll one end firmly to form the tail. Lengthen the body by rolling it in the palm of your hand. The overall length will be about 10cm (4in). Make a dip for the head by pressing a finger in.

7 With the body lying on its side, dampen and attach one back leg and one front leg slightly under the body. Attach the other two legs and lay Cattie across a straight line to make sure that all her feet are in line, so that she will be able to stand up when she is dry. Support between the legs to keep them apart while drying.

8 Dampen the dip and attach the head to the body.

9 Mix a little of each of the colour powders with a few drops of vodka, then paint on the markings. Do not stand Cattie up until she is completely dry.

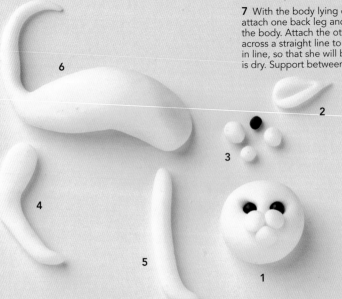

Cattie is my nephew and niece's family cat. She spends her time hiding from the family dog, Mr Tibbs.

Snowball

Materials:

15g (½oz) white modelling paste

2 x black sugar pearls

Small amount of pink fondant (sugarpaste)

Tools:

Dresden tool

Small, fine palette knife

Instructions:

1 Shape 5g (¹/₆oz) of modelling paste into a ball. Mark two holes for the eyes using the Dresden tool and insert the black sugar pearl eyes.

2 Make two ears by shaping very small balls of white paste, and two smaller balls of pink fondant (sugarpaste) into pointed cone shapes. Press each pink cone on top of the white cone, then press the wide end of the Dresden tool in to make a dip in the middle. Dampen and attach the ears to the back of the head.

3 Make three very small balls of white paste for the cheeks and chin, and shape a tiny piece of pink fondant (sugarpaste) for the nose.

4 Attach all four pieces to the face.

5 Shape the rest of the paste (about 10g/¹/₃oz) into an oval to make the body.

6 Pinch one end up firmly to form the short tail.

7 Pinch and shape four small legs as shown. Mark three toes onto the front feet with the knife. Make a dip for the head by by pressing a finger in.

8 Dampen the dip and attach the head, slightly cocked to one side.

32

Snowball is always ready for fun and a
toy mouse is her favourite plaything!

Buster

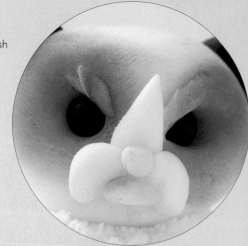

Materials:

20g (²/₃oz) white modelling paste

5g (¹/₆oz) dark brown modelling paste

Small amount of white fondant (sugarpaste)

2 x black sugar pearls

Tiny piece of pink fondant (sugarpaste)

Dark brown food colour powder

Cocktail stick (optional)

Tools:

Dresden tool

Small paintbrush

Small, fine palette knife

Tea strainer or small sieve

Instructions:

1 Shape 5g (¹/₆oz) of modelling paste into an oval. Mark two holes for the eyes using the Dresden tool and insert the black sugar pearl eyes.

2 Make two tiny sausages of white modelling paste for the eyebrows. Dampen the area above the eyes and attach them, angled down in the middle, to give Buster an angry expression. Brush dark brown food colour powder around the eyes.

3 Make two very small ovals of white modelling paste for the cheeks, and one small ball for the chin. Dampen the face and attach with the cheeks drooping down and the chin pushed up to make Buster look grumpy.

4 Shape a tiny cone of white and attach it to the face, then stick on a tiny pink nose.

5 Make two ears as described on page 8. Dampen and attach them to the back of the head.

6 Make a curved, dark brown tail approximately 3cm (1¼in) long.

7 Cut a 5g (¹/₆oz) piece of paste into four pieces, and shape the two back legs first by making two 2cm (¾in) cones.

8 Shape the front legs into 4cm (1½in) sausages, slightly bent at the end. Mark three toes onto all four feet with a knife. Brush dark brown food colour powder, leaving the feet white.

9 Shape the rest of the paste (about 10g/¹/₃oz) into a cone about 4cm (1½in) long to make the body. If you want to provide extra support for the head, push a cocktail stick into the body, but remember to warn people that there is a stick inside. Brush on dark brown food colour powder over Buster's back.

10 Attach the back legs and tail under the body.

11 Attach the head to the body and stick the front legs on.

12 Press a small amount of white fondant (sugarpaste) through a tea strainer or small sieve. Cut the fluff off and attach to Buster's chest, as described on page 12.

Buster is not a cat to be messed with. He is a very independent character who can be a bit grumpy, but also has an affectionate side.

Cordelia

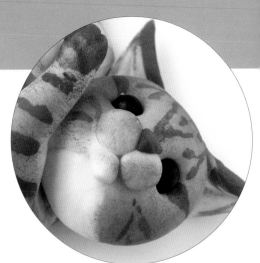

Materials:

20g (²/₃oz) cream
   modelling paste

2 x black sugar pearls

Tiny piece of brown
   fondant (sugarpaste)

Dark brown food colour powder

Vodka for painting

Small amount of blue
   fondant (sugarpaste)

Tools:

Dresden tool

Small
   paintbrush

Small, fine
   palette knife

Instructions:

1 Shape 5g (¹/₆oz) of modelling paste into a ball, mark two holes for the eyes using the Dresden tool and insert the black sugar pearl eyes.

2 Make two ears as described on page 8. Dampen and attach them to the back of the head.

3 Make three very small balls of paste for the cheeks and chin and attach them to the face. Attach a tiny piece of brown fondant (sugarpaste) for the nose.

4 Cordelia's head is now complete.

5 Cut a 5g (¹/₆oz) piece of paste into four pieces, and shape the two back legs first by making two 3cm (1¼in) cones. Bend them in the middle and flatten the wide end slightly.

6 Shape the front legs into 3cm (1¼in) sausages and bend them in the middle. Mark three toes onto all four feet with the knife.

7 Shape the rest of the paste (about 10g/¹/₃oz) into a ball, then roll one end firmly to form the tail.

Lengthen the body by rolling it in the palm of your hand. The overall length will be about 10cm (4in). Make it into a curved shape, then make a dip at the wide end for the head by pressing a finger in.

8 Dampen and attach both back legs, one leg under the body and one on top. Then attach both front legs.

9 Dampen the dip and attach the head to the body.

10 Shape the blue fondant (sugarpaste) into a rounded cone shape to make a tiny mouse and position it between Cordelia's paws.

11 Brush some dark brown food colour powder over Cordelia, avoiding her tummy and chin. Mix a little of the powder with a few drops of vodka, then paint on the markings.

Cordelia is named after a Swedish friend, who made sure that the first Swedish word I learned was katt!

Livvi

Materials:

20g (²/₃oz) beige modelling paste

10g (¹/₃oz) black modelling paste

Black food colour powder

Vodka for painting

Cocktail stick (optional)

Tools:

Dresden tool

Small paintbrush

Small, fine palette knife

Instructions:

1 Shape 5g (¹/₆oz) of beige modelling paste into a ball. Roll one side of the ball to form a short pear shape – the narrow end becomes the front of the face. Mark two lines using the Dresden tool to make the closed eyes.

2 Make two ears as described on page 8. Dampen and attach the ears to the back of the head.

3 Make one small oval of the beige paste for the chin and stick in place.

4 Shape a tiny piece of black paste for the nose and attach it to the face.

5 Cut a 5g (¹/₆oz) piece of black paste into four pieces, and shape the two back legs first by making two 2cm (¾in) cones.

6 Shape the front legs into 3cm (1¼in) sausages. Mark three toes onto all four feet with the knife.

7 Make a long, thin tail using a small piece of black modelling paste.

8 Shape about 10g (¹/₃oz) of the beige paste into a cone about 4cm (1½in) long, to make the body. If you want to provide extra support for the head, push a cocktail stick into the body, but remember to warn people that there is a stick inside.

9 Attach the back legs and tail under the body. Attach the head to the body, slightly turned to one side.

10 Use the dry paintbrush to brush black food colour powder over the front of the face and down Livvi's back. Mix a little of the powder with a few drops of vodka, then paint the eyelids.

11 Shape a large pea-sized piece of beige paste into a cone shape and flatten it slightly until it is wide enough to cover the top half of the legs. Stick it in place, and then mark it with the Dresden tool to make a fur effect.

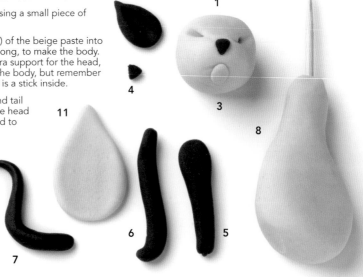

Livvi is a sociable Siamese cat who likes human company, is very intelligent and doesn't like to be alone.

Asher

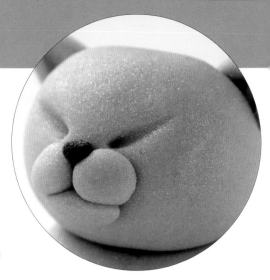

Materials:

20g (²/₃oz) grey sugar modelling paste

Tiny piece of black fondant (sugarpaste)

Grey food colour powder mixed with a little pearl white

Tools:

Dresden tool

Small paintbrush

Small, fine palette knife

Instructions:

1 To make the head, shape 5g (¹/₆oz) of modelling paste into a ball. Mark two lines for the eyes using the Dresden tool.

2 Make two ears as described on page 8. Dampen and attach the ears to the back of the head.

3 Make two very small ovals of paste for the cheeks, one small ball for the chin and shape a tiny piece of black fondant (sugarpaste) for the nose.

4 Attach all four pieces to Asher's face.

5 Cut a 5g (¹/₆oz) piece of paste into four pieces for the legs, and shape them into 2cm (¾in) cones. Mark three toes onto each foot with the knife. Curve two of the pieces to form the front legs.

6 Shape the rest of the paste (about 10g/¹/₃oz) into a ball to make the body, and then roll one end firmly to form the tail. The overall length will be about 7cm (2¾in). Press a finger in at the head end to make a dip, and mark the top of the back leg with the Dresden tool.

7 Dampen the legs and stick them under the body. Curve the tail around the body. Dampen the dip at the front of the body and attach Asher's head.

8 Use a dry paintbrush to dust the grey pearl food colour powder all over the cat.

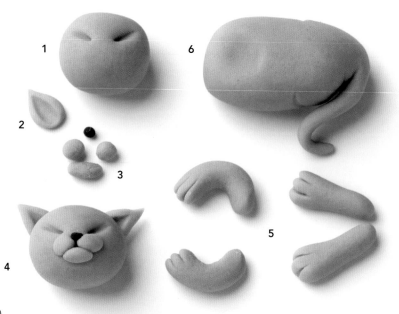

Asher is my own smug British Blue cat. She has an amazing range of facial expressions and can shout at the top of her voice at 5am to get attention!

Sasha

Materials:

20g (²/₃oz) black modelling paste

Small amount of white modelling paste

2 x black sugar pearls

Tiny piece of pink fondant (sugarpaste)

Tools:

Dresden tool

Small, fine palette knife

Small foam pieces

Instructions:

1 Shape 5g (¹/₆oz)of black modelling paste into a ball. Mark two holes for the eyes using the Dresden tool and insert the black sugar pearl eyes.

2 Make two ears as described on page 8. Dampen and attach the ears to the back of the head.

3 Make three very small balls for the cheeks and chin using white modelling paste and shape a tiny piece of pink fondant (sugarpaste) for the nose.

4 Stick all four pieces onto the face.

5 Cut a 3g (¹/₈oz) piece of black paste in half, and shape the two back legs by making two 4cm (1½in) cones. Bend the legs in the middle and flatten the wide end slightly.

6 Shape the rest of the black paste (about 12g/²/₅oz) into a ball, then roll one end firmly to form the tail and roll the other end for the front. Lengthen the body by rolling it in the palm of your hand. The overall length will be about 10cm (4in).

7 Cut 3cm (1¼in) into the front end of the body for the front legs with the palette knife and curl Sasha's tail over her back. Make a dip at the front for the head by pushing a finger in.

8 Attach a very small ball of white paste to each leg for the paws. Mark three toes onto all four paws with the knife. Shape a tiny ball of white paste into a sausage and attach it to the tip of the tail.

9 Dampen the dip and attach the head to the body.

10 Support the body at the back end with the foam pieces while it is drying. Attach the back legs, and position the body so that Sasha will stand up when dry.

Sasha is a young, active cat who is enjoying having a stretch after her long sleep.

Coco

Materials:

20g (²/₃oz) brown modelling paste

Small amount of brown fondant (sugarpaste)

2 x black sugar pearls

Tiny piece of black fondant (sugarpaste)

Tools:

Dresden tool

Small, fine palette knife

Tea strainer or small sieve

Instructions:

1 Shape 5g (¹/₆oz) of modelling paste into an oval to make the head. Mark two holes for the eyes using the Dresden tool and insert the black sugar pearl eyes.

2 Make two ears as described on page 8. Dampen and attach the ears to the back of the head.

3 Make three very small balls of brown modelling paste for the cheeks and chin, and shape a tiny piece of black fondant (sugarpaste) for the nose.

4 Attach all four pieces to the face.

5 Cut a 5g (¹/₆oz) piece of brown modelling paste into four pieces, and shape the two back legs first by making two 4cm (1½in) cones. Bend in the middle and flatten the wide end slightly.

6 Shape the front legs into 3cm (1¼in) sausages. Mark three toes onto all four feet with the knife.

7 Shape the rest of the paste (about 10g/¹/₃oz) into a ball to make the body, then roll one end firmly to form the tail. Lengthen the body by rolling it in the palm of your hand. The overall length will be about 10cm (4in). Make a dip for the head by pressing a finger in.

8 Dampen and attach one back leg slightly under the body and the other above it. Then attach the two front legs pointing forwards.

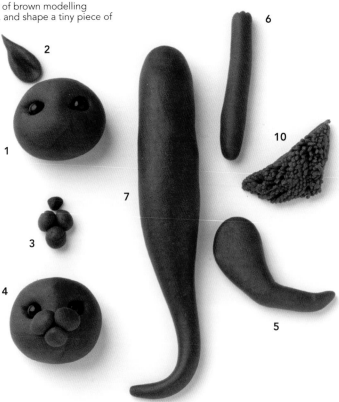

9 Dampen the dip and attach the head to the body.

10 Press a small amount of brown fondant (sugarpaste) through the tea strainer or small sieve. Cut the fluff off and attach it to Coco's chest, as described on page 12.

Coco is a beautiful chocolate brown cat, shown in a very serene pose enjoying a rest after his playtime.

Raskal

Materials:

20g (²/₃oz) black modelling paste

Small amount of vegetable oil (optional)

Tools:

Dresden tool

Small, fine palette knife

Instructions:

1 Shape 5g (¹/₆oz) of modelling paste into a ball to make the head and mark two lines for the closed eyes using the Dresden tool.

2 Make two ears as described on page 8. Dampen and attach the ears to the back of the head.

3 Make two very small balls of paste for the cheeks, one small oval for the chin and shape a tiny piece of paste for the nose.

4 Attach all four pieces to the face.

5 Cut a 5g (¹/₆oz) piece of paste into four pieces, and shape the legs into 3cm (1¼in) sausages. Mark three toes onto each foot with the knife.

6 Shape the rest of the paste (about 10g/¹/₃oz) into a ball to make the body.

7 Roll one end firmly to form the tail. Lengthen the body by rolling it in the palm of your hand. The overall length will be about 10cm (4in). Make a dip for the head by pressing a finger in.

8 Attach the legs as shown in the photograph opposite, so that Raskal is lying on his back with his legs in the air.

9 Dampen the dip and attach the head to the body.

10 Black modelling paste can look a bit dull and matt, so if you want Raskal to look more shiny, put a few drops of vegetable oil on a piece of kitchen paper and lightly wipe over the surface of the cat.

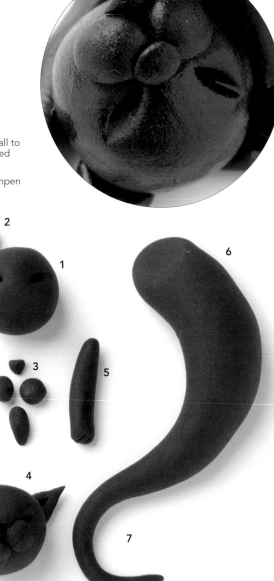

46

Raskal was a real character with a fantastic
shiny black coat, who strutted around like he
owned the place but was very gentle when
he came to live with my cats. He particularly
loved playing with kittens.

Acknowledgements
My thanks go to the team at Search Press,
including May Corfield and Sophie Kersey
for their editorial support, Paul Bricknell
for the beautiful photography, and
Marrianne Miall for styling the photographs.

Publisher's Note
You are invited to visit the author's website:
www.franklysweet.co.uk